Cornerstones of Freedom

Civil Rights Marches

LINDA and CHARLES GEORGE

CHILDREN'S PRESS®
A Division of Grolier Publishing
New York • London • Hong Kong • Sydney
Danbury, Connecticut

Visit Children's Press on the Internet at:
http://publishing.grolier.com

Library of Congress Cataloging-in-Publication Data

George, Linda.
  Civil rights marches / Linda and Charles George.
    p. cm.—(Cornerstones of freedom)
  Includes index.
  Summary: Describes the peaceful marches in the United States on behalf
of civil rights for blacks from the 1950s to the 1990s, including the March on
Washington and other important marches.
  ISBN: 0-516-21183-8 (lib. bdg.)   0-516-26516-4 (pbk.)
  1. Afro-Americans—Civil rights—History—20th century—Juvenile
literature. 2. Civil rights demonstrations—United States—History—20th
century—Juvenile literature. 3. United States—Race relations—Juvenile
literature. [1. Afro-Americans—Civil rights. 2. Civil rights movements.
3. Race relations.] I. George, Charles, 1949–. II. Title. III. Series.
E185.61.G29 1999
973`.0496073—dc21
                                                      98-41943
                                                          CIP
                                                          AC

Names such as Jesus of Nazareth, Henry David Thoreau, and Mahatma Gandhi are not usually associated with the American civil rights marches of the 1950s and 1960s. But these men taught about the power of love, nonviolence, and civil disobedience (disobeying laws believed to be cruel or unjust). Such powerful ideas were recognized by Martin Luther King Jr. and other black leaders. They believed these ideas could bring change that was badly needed to achieve freedom for all people.

Martin Luther King Jr. was a young pastor when this photograph was taken in 1955.

This photograph of students in a crowded segregated classroom was taken in 1961.

The 1950s and 1960s were a time when laws in the American South prevented black children from going to school with white children. Black children attended segregated, or separate, schools that were sometimes small and unheated. Often, their books and sports equipment were castoffs from white schools. School bus transportation was available only to white children. Black children could not use public libraries, swimming pools, or parks.

Good jobs were not available for many black adults. They had to settle for menial work as maids, porters, and laborers. Black adults were not allowed to vote. They had no voice in the election of officials who passed laws governing their lives.

Many of the laws maintained the separation of the races. Throughout the South, at public places such as movie theaters, drinking fountains, and

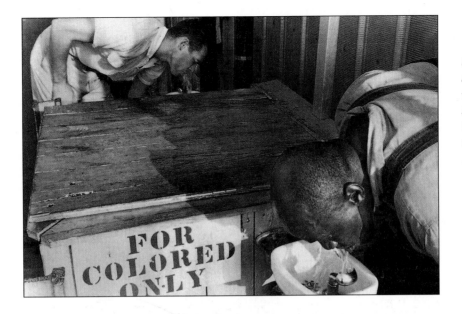

restrooms, signs read "For Whites Only" or "For Colored Only."

By the 1960s, one hundred years had passed since the Emancipation Proclamation of 1863 freed the slaves. Yet black people in the United States still did not enjoy true equality or freedom. In 1954, the U.S. Supreme Court ruled to end segregation in public schools. This, however, did not bring about the changes black Americans knew they deserved as citizens of this country. Black leaders called for direct action. They believed that if true justice was to exist in the United States, black citizens should be responsible for establishing it. But many black leaders wondered what form of action to take. They knew that violence would only convince some white Americans that their long-held ideas about black people were correct. Something more powerful was required.

Martin Luther King Jr. wrote in *The Strength to Love,* published in 1963, "Returning hate for hate multiplies hate, adding deeper darkness to a night already devoid of stars. Darkness cannot drive out darkness; only light can do that. Hate cannot drive out hate; only love can do that." Dr. King and other black leaders began a national campaign of public marches. Black leaders wanted white Americans to recognize injustice in the country. The peaceful demonstrators were a powerful contrast to the cruelty and violence of police dogs, tear gas, fire hoses, and mass arrests that often resulted from the demonstrations. This soon led to moral outrage nationwide and a change in attitudes toward blacks.

A group of black demonstrators begin to assemble outside a segregated restaurant.

Martin Luther King Jr.'s philosophy of nonviolence was a combination of ideas. The teachings of Jesus of Nazareth, the writings of Henry David Thoreau, and the beliefs and methods of Mahatma Gandhi were the most important. As a child in Atlanta, Georgia, King listened as his father preached sermons about the love of Jesus. He knew how powerful Christian love could be, but love had not been enough in the American South.

As a student at Morehouse College, King read works by Henry David Thoreau (1817–62) about civil disobedience. Thoreau had gone to prison to protest the U.S. government's support of slavery before the Civil War (1861–65). King was moved by the idea of refusing to cooperate with unfair laws.

Henry David Thoreau was an American writer who wrote mostly about nature, but held strong views about injustice in society.

In 1948, King was attending Crozer Theological Seminary. In Philadelphia, Pennsylvania, he attended a lecture that centered on the philosophy and actions of Mahatma Gandhi (1869–1948), who had led the people of India in their fight against British rule.

Mahatma Gandhi was killed on January 30, 1948, by an opponent of his nonviolent philosophy.

The lecturer told the crowd about how Gandhi, a man of no particular importance, had inspired an entire nation. Gandhi taught nonviolence. He spent time in jail, and went without food for long periods of time as a form of protest. He told his followers not to raise a hand against the British forces. King was especially moved by the Indian leader's famous 1930 Salt March to the Sea. To protest England's monopoly on the production of salt in his country, Gandhi led thousands of followers to the sea. They broke the law by making their own salt.

King was deeply impressed by Gandhi's other nonviolent tactics, which included boycotts and strikes. He was inspired by Gandhi's belief in love as an instrument for overcoming evil. King called this philosophy "the most potent weapon available to an oppressed people in the struggle for freedom."

In June 1955, Martin Luther King Jr. earned his Doctor of Philosophy degree in Theology, the study of religion, from Boston University. On a cold December day that same year, Rosa Parks refused to give up her seat to a white person on a Montgomery, Alabama, bus. She was arrested. Dr. King decided to use this incident as an opportunity to put the philosophy of nonviolence to the test.

Rosa Parks

Speaking before his congregation at Holt Street Baptist Church in Montgomery, Dr. King said, "There comes a time when people get tired of being trampled over by the iron feet of oppression. . . . We are not here advocating violence. We have overcome that. We are a Christian people. . . . The only weapon that we have in our hands this evening is the weapon of protest." The church was packed with people and four thousand more listeners were in the street outside. King continued: "One of the great glories of democracy is the right to protest for right. . . . We will be guided by the highest principles of law and order. . . . If you will protest courageously and yet with dignity and Christian love, when the history books are written in future generations, the historians will have to pause and say: 'There lived a great people—a black people—who injected new meaning and dignity into the veins of civilization.' This is our challenge and our overwhelming responsibility."

Martin Luther King Jr. addresses the congregation at Holt Street Baptist Church in Montgomery, Alabama.

Dr. King and other black leaders began a mission of nonviolent civil disobedience, using marches and demonstrations. They knew the time had come for black Americans to assume full citizenship under the Declaration of Independence, which promises that "all men are created equal."

Dr. King recognized Rosa Parks's actions as a chance to gain the attention of the nation. He called on black citizens to refuse to ride the buses in Montgomery until blacks were allowed to sit wherever they chose. After twelve months, the boycott achieved its goal. Buses in Montgomery were desegregated. The nation watched and waited for the next step.

In this April 26, 1956, photograph, demonstrators cheer as King (at podium) announces that the five-month-old Montgomery Bus Boycott will continue until Montgomery buses are completely desegregated.

*President Dwight
D. Eisenhower*

In 1957, a new group was formed called the Southern Christian Leadership Conference (SCLC). Their first act was to organize a nationwide demonstration, called a Prayer Pilgrimage, in Washington, D.C. The newly formed SCLC sent a telegram to President Dwight D. Eisenhower. In it, the SCLC requested that the president hold a White House conference on civil rights. Eisenhower denied the request.

The SCLC then chose May 17, 1957, as the day their march on Washington would take place. This date was chosen because it was the third anniversary of the Supreme Court's decision to abolish segregation in schools.

Organizers from the National Association for the Advancement of Colored People (NAACP) invited black ministers from throughout the South, and their congregations, to come to Washington to "pray for freedom on the steps of the Lincoln Memorial." An estimated thirty thousand people from thirty-three states came to Washington that day.

A. Philip Randolph, a long-time fighter for civil rights, led the activities that day. For more than three hours, he introduced many speakers. The crowd became restless. Martin Luther King Jr. worried that everyone would be too tired to hear what he had to say. But the crowd had become restless waiting for

A. Philip Randolph

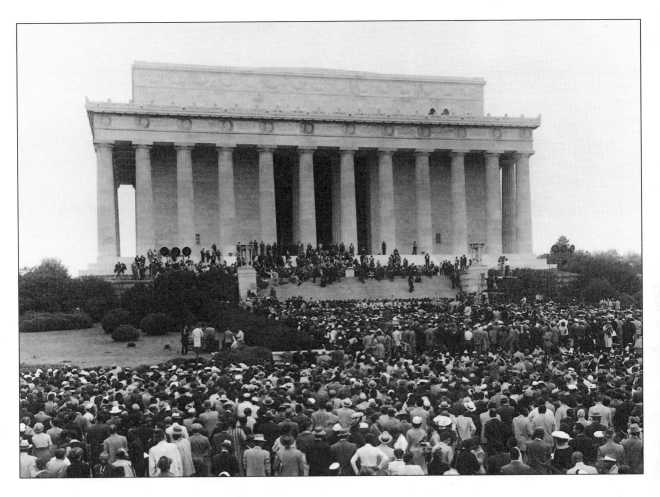

his speech. Finally, Randolph introduced him.

Dressed in a flowing black clergyman's robe, Dr. King spoke about voting rights. "So long as I do not firmly . . . possess the right to vote, I do not possess myself." Dr. King's impassioned plea for voting rights for black Americans ended with a call for strong leadership from the federal government. Dr. King asked for help from both the Republican and Democrat parties, as well as from the black community.

Part of the crowd at the Lincoln Memorial for the May 17, 1957, Prayer Pilgrimage

The Prayer Pilgrimage gained support for new civil rights laws. As a result, Congress passed the first major civil rights law since Reconstruction (1865–77), following the Civil War. The law established a Civil Rights Commission, which gave federal protection to blacks who wanted to vote.

After the Prayer Pilgrimage, Dr. King became the leader of the Civil Rights Movement in the United States. The *Amsterdam News* of New York City said, "At this point in his career, the people will follow him anywhere."

By 1963, nonviolent resistance was gaining more attention throughout the United States. The campaign that had been launched on a massive scale with the year-long Montgomery Bus Boycott in 1955–56 expanded. Student sit-ins, in which black college students would refuse to leave a segregated restaurant until they received service, began in the early 1960s. The Freedom Rides of 1961, in which a group of

In this famous 1960 photograph, four black college students conduct a sit-in at a lunch counter in Greensboro, North Carolina. They refused to leave until they were served.

blacks and whites rode buses through the South from Washington, D.C., to New Orleans, Louisiana, defied segregationist rules. Nonviolent direct action had become a powerful weapon in the movement for black freedom.

In May 1963, the nation focused its attention on Birmingham, Alabama. Martin Luther King Jr. had called it "the most segregated city in America," and he chose it for a major series of demonstrations. Marches, boycotts, and sit-ins were planned to try to win desegregation of stores, restaurants, and other public places. When the police arrived, some of the black demonstrators were attacked by snarling German shepherds. Others were hurled against buildings by stinging jets of water. These images were carried across the nation on television. As a result, many whites began to understand the often brutal rules of segregation.

Black demonstrators attempt to shield themselves as firemen hose them with water to break up their gathering. This photograph was taken in Birmingham, Alabama, on May 4, 1963.

Even blacks who served in the United States military had to endure racial segregation.

COLORED
WAITING ROOM
INTRASTATE PASSENGERS →

PULLMAN PASSENGERS
CHECK WITH PULLMAN
CONDUCTOR AT RECEIVING
TABLE BEFORE GOING TO
TRAINS 4-11 & 36
CARS 7-40-54-0145-58

Horrified by the images of the violence in Birmingham, President John F. Kennedy sent a civil rights bill to Congress in June to end segregation in hotels, restaurants, theaters, and all public places. It also gave the Justice Department the power to sue school districts that refused to desegregate. To urge Congress to pass the bill, A. Philip Randolph proposed another march on Washington to unite people behind the historic law.

On August 28, 1963, nearly 250,000 people from almost every state in the Union gathered at the Lincoln Memorial. Eighty million Americans viewed the event on television. They heard the intelligent, informed, thoughtful words of black spokesmen from all walks of life. Many saw clearly for the first time the truth behind black Americans' struggle for equal treatment.

For one day, thousands of Americans walked together, ate together, laughed together, and cried together. Not one ugly incident spoiled the day. As Martin Luther King Jr. wrote in 1964, "It was an army without guns, but not without strength. . . . [Followers] of every faith, members of every class, every profession, every political party [were] united by a single ideal."

By late afternoon, the marchers were tired. But when Randolph introduced "the moral leader of our nation," the crowd came alive.

This aerial photograph shows the mass of participants in the March on Washington that was held on August 28, 1963.

Dr. King began slowly and formally, presenting his prepared speech. As he spoke, the crowd responded with great emotion. Dr. King soon forgot about the speech he had written. Instead, he told the world about his dream of justice— a world without color barriers. His desire for equality and freedom touched the hearts of all who heard it. His speech continues to inspire people today.

"Even though we face the difficulties of today and tomorrow, I still have a dream. It is a dream deeply rooted in the American dream. I have a dream that one day this nation will rise up and live out the true meaning of its creed, 'We hold these truths to be self-evident that all men are created equal.' . . ."

Martin Luther King Jr. addresses the crowd at the Lincoln Memorial.

"And when we allow freedom to ring from every village, from every hamlet, from every state and every city, we will be able to join hands and sing . . . 'Free at last, free at last. Thank God Almighty, we're free at last!' "

There was a moment of silence at the end of the speech. Then people cheered wildly. Many wept. The power of King's speech lay in the voice it gave to the hope of twenty-two million black Americans. Later that day, Dr. King and the other leaders of the march met with President Kennedy at the White House. Kennedy praised "the deep fervor and quiet dignity of the marchers."

After the march, King (second from left) and A. Philip Randolph (second from right) met with President Kennedy (right) at the White House.

President Kennedy did not live to see the civil rights bill become law. He was shot and killed

President Lyndon Johnson (seated) signed the civil rights bill into law on July 2, 1964. (Martin Luther King Jr. is standing directly behind Johnson.)

in Dallas, Texas, on November 22, 1963. President Lyndon B. Johnson used his influence in Congress to insure the passage of the bill. On July 2, 1964, Martin Luther King Jr., along with other proud civil rights leaders, watched President Johnson sign the bill into law.

King and other leaders then shifted their concerns from the desegregation of public places to voting rights. Blacks in some areas of the South were not registered to vote. The United States Constitution gave them the right to vote, but most did not register. Many black people had received threats and feared whites would hurt them if they registered. Some feared losing their jobs. Still others could not pass the reading requirements necessary to register. In Mississippi, for example, blacks had to explain difficult sections of the state's constitution in order to vote. White voting officials made sure they never passed the tests.

In 1965, the push for voter registration

increased. Selma, Alabama, became the target city. Mass meetings were held. On February 1, Dr. King, along with Ralph Abernathy, vice president and treasurer of the SCLC, led a march to the courthouse. They and three hundred others were arrested for parading without a permit.

Dr. King announced there would be a 54-mile (87-kilometer) march from Selma to the state capitol in Montgomery on March 7. Alabama Governor George Wallace issued an order prohibiting the march. Black leaders in Selma announced that the march would go ahead as planned.

Civil rights protesters on their march from Selma, Alabama, to the state capitol in Montgomery.

March 7, 1965, has become known as "Bloody Sunday." Hosea Williams of the SCLC and John Lewis of the Student Nonviolent Coordinating Committee (SNCC) led 525 marchers out of Brown's Chapel Methodist Church in Selma and over the Edmund Pettus Bridge. A chill wind stung their faces as they crossed the bridge. They came face-to-face with the sheriff and more than fifty state troopers armed with clubs, whips, and gas masks. The marchers were ordered to turn around. No one moved.

Seconds later, the sheriff gave the order for the troopers to advance. Marchers were clubbed, whipped, choked with tear gas, and chased back across the bridge. Unarmed and defeated, they stumbled away from the "battlefield."

Some whites on the sidelines cheered as dozens of men, women, and children staggered blindly or fell wounded. Sixteen people had to be hospitalized. Forty others were treated and released from the hospital. A hundred more limped home.

The events at Selma, recorded by newspapers and television, affected the entire country. Public reaction was swift. People from all over the United States rushed to Selma to march alongside the black demonstrators.

On Monday, March 15, President Johnson expressed his anger to the nation about the events that took place in Selma: "It is wrong—

deadly wrong—to deny any of your fellow
Americans the right to vote in this country. It is
the effort of American Negroes to secure for
themselves the full blessing of American life.
Their cause must be our cause, too."

*A state patrol
sergeant helps
load an injured
demonstrator into
an ambulance after
police broke up
the march.*

In this March 21, 1965, photograph, thousands of marchers stream across the Edmund Pettus Bridge on the march to Montgomery.

On Sunday, March 21, 1965, a second march from Selma to Montgomery began. Martin Luther King Jr., leading more than two thousand marchers and protected by three thousand federal troops and United States helicopters, left Selma on a historic five-day march.

Obeying a court order to insure the safety of the marchers, all but three hundred left the procession after 8 miles (13 km). For five days, the eyes of the nation were once again focused on the South. The events in Alabama demonstrated that new laws were needed to protect the voting rights of all citizens.

Martin Luther King Jr. leads supporters on their five-day march from Selma to Montgomery.

On Thursday, March 25, nearly twenty-five thousand people from across the nation gathered outside Montgomery to join the marchers. With Dr. King in the lead, they covered the last 3 miles (5 km) to the state capitol. Governor Wallace refused to accept the marchers' petition for voting rights and watched from his office window.

At the end of the day, Dr. King stood before the capitol and addressed the crowd. "I know some of you are asking today, 'How long will it take?' I come to say to you this afternoon however difficult the moment, however frustrating the hour, it will not be long, because truth pressed to earth will rise again. . . . How long? Not long, because the arm of the moral universe is long

Dr. King speaking in front of the Alabama state capitol after the completion of the march on March 25, 1965.

but it bends toward justice." Later, Dr. King called the Selma march "the most powerful and dramatic civil rights protest that has ever taken place in the South."

Just a few months later, the Voting Rights Act was signed into law, granting all black citizens the right to vote. The act remains the crowning achievement of the Civil Rights Movement.

Across the South, black voter registration more than tripled in only a few years. Today, there are thousands of black elected officials nationwide, including congressmen, senators, and mayors. The success of the Selma campaign marked the climax of the Civil Rights Movement in the South.

A state official helps a black voter register as others wait their turn. This photograph was taken in Canton, Mississippi, on January 15, 1966.

Today, Martin Luther King Jr.'s vision, and the example set by the Civil Rights Movement of the 1950s and 1960s, still inspire people. By exposing injustice to blacks, other injustices throughout American society were revealed. Oppressed people throughout the world use the success of the American movement as the model to overcome their own struggles.

The actions of the brave men and women of the Civil Rights Movement succeeded because of the influence of the nonviolent leaders who came before them. They stressed the humanity of all people, regardless of race. Even though Martin Luther King Jr., who was assassinated in 1968, and others died in pursuit of civil rights, their influence on the leaders who follow them continues.

As King lies mortally wounded on the balcony of the Lorraine Motel in Memphis, Tennessee, witnesses point in the direction of the gunshots that later killed him. This photograph was taken on April 4, 1968.

OTHER CIVIL RIGHTS MARCHES IN WASHINGTON, D.C.

1958 Youth March for Integrated Schools

About ten thousand demonstrators marched down Constitution Avenue toward the Lincoln Memorial. Most were college students, but some were as young as fourth graders. They were led by "Mr. Civil Rights," A. Philip Randolph and Coretta Scott King, wife of Martin Luther King Jr.

1959 Second Youth March on Washington

About twenty-five thousand marchers participated. Martin Luther King Jr., Roy Wilkins of the NAACP, and Tom Mboya, the leader of Kenya, spoke.

1977 National Organization for Women (NOW)

Four thousand people marched down Pennsylvania Avenue to demand ratification of the Equal Rights Amendment.

1993 National March on Washington for Lesbian, Gay, Bisexual, and Transgendered Rights

About 750,000 marchers were in attendance.

GLOSSARY

Rosa Parks's arrest led to the Montgomery Bus Boycott.

Martin Luther King Jr. was a civil rights leader.

boycott – to refuse to buy something or take part in something as a way of protesting

brutality – cruelty and violence

castoffs – items that someone else has thrown away

civil disobedience – disobeying laws believed to be cruel or unjust

civil rights – individual rights that all members of a society have to freedom and equal treatment under the law

climax – the most exciting part of an event

democracy – way of governing a country in which the people choose their leaders in elections

desegregate – to do away with the practice of separating people of different races in schools, restaurants, and other public places

dignity – quality or manner worthy of honor or respect

fervor – strong or intense feeling

menial – lowly, lacking interest or dignity

monopoly – the complete control of something, especially a service or the supply of a product

oppression – being treated in a cruel, unjust, and harsh way

porter – person who carries luggage for people at railroad stations or hotels, also a person who waits on train passengers

strike – refusal to work because of an argument or a disagreement with an employer over wages or working conditions

tactics – plans or methods to achieve a goal

TIMELINE

May 17: U.S. Supreme Court abolishes segregation in public schools

1954

1955 *December 1:* Rosa Parks is arrested in Montgomery, Alabama
December 5: Montgomery Bus Boycott begins

1956 *December 21:* Montgomery Bus Boycott ends

1957 *February 14:* SCLC founded
May 17: Prayer Pilgrimage for Freedom in Washington, D.C.
August 29: Congress passes first civil rights legislation since Reconstruction

1963 *April 3:* Birmingham, Alabama, demonstrations begin
August 28: March on Washington for Jobs and Freedom
November 22: President Kennedy assassinated; Johnson becomes president

July 2: President Johnson signs civil rights bill **1964**

1965 *March 7:* "Bloody Sunday" in Selma, Alabama
March 21–25: Selma-to-Montgomery march to demand voting rights
August 4: President Johnson signs Voting Rights Act

1968 *April 4:* Martin Luther King Jr. assassinated

INDEX *(Boldface page numbers indicate illustrations.)*

PHOTO CREDITS

ABOUT THE AUTHORS

Charles and Linda George are former teachers who have authored more than two dozen nonfiction books for children and young adults. For Children's Press, they have written for series including Cornerstones of Freedom, Community Builders, and America the Beautiful, Second Series.

Mr. and Mrs. George have been married since 1971, have two children, Christy and Alex, and live in central Texas near the small town of Rising Star. They enjoy traveling in their travel trailer to do research and gather ideas for new projects.